One Day in the Life of
DANIEL RADCLIFFE
January 13 2009 New York City

TIM HAILAND

Dan and I first met while he was starring as Alan Strang, a troubled stable boy, in the London revival of the Peter Shaffer play EQUUS, in 2007. It was great to see how he grew as a performer in the time between the London and Broadway runs. As I got to know Dan, I experienced what a smart, sensitive, and above all, curious person he is. We struck up a friendship which has resulted in this book of images that you now hold.

On January 13, 2009, I arrived at Dan's Manhattan apartment at 10:10 am, and with camera in hand, started recording his day from start to finish. The television in his bedroom was on from the night before. Upon waking, Dan told me that he likes to watch cartoons in the morning. Then, breakfast, showering, getting dressed, an acting lesson, an afternoon rehearsal for the intense blinding scene in EQUUS, the evening performance itself, and signing autographs for the slew of fans that wait for him every night outside the stage door. Over the course of the day we talked about movies and music, as we often do; I told Dan how Morrissey's band the Smiths changed my life, and he told me how Pete Doherty's group the Libertines changed his. I also asked him if he had ever thought of directing films—given his curious mind and analytical nature, I think he would be very good at it. Dan said that he is, in fact, interested in working behind the camera someday. At 11:00 p.m., we drive back home, hopping out into the cold night air of Times Square, one of my favorite places to do a portrait session, along the way. Finally, Dan went home to his apartment, where he got back into bed. One Day in the Life, one daily ritual: waking from the private world of sleep, doing lots of colorful and not-so-colorful things in the big world, then back to the seclusion and privacy of one's bed. It's what we all do, every day.

Though Dan is known to millions worldwide for his portrayal of Harry Potter on the big screen, hopefully these pictures will give you greater insight into his life, the life of a gifted and hard-working actor. He's a very inspiring person, and a pleasure to spend a day with. I hope to be more like Dan when I grow up.

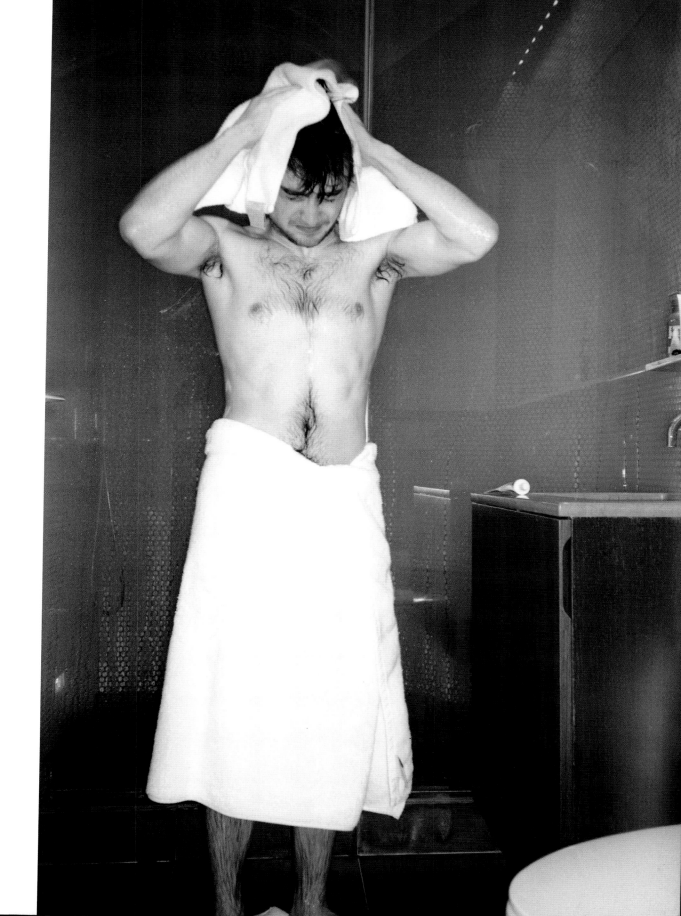

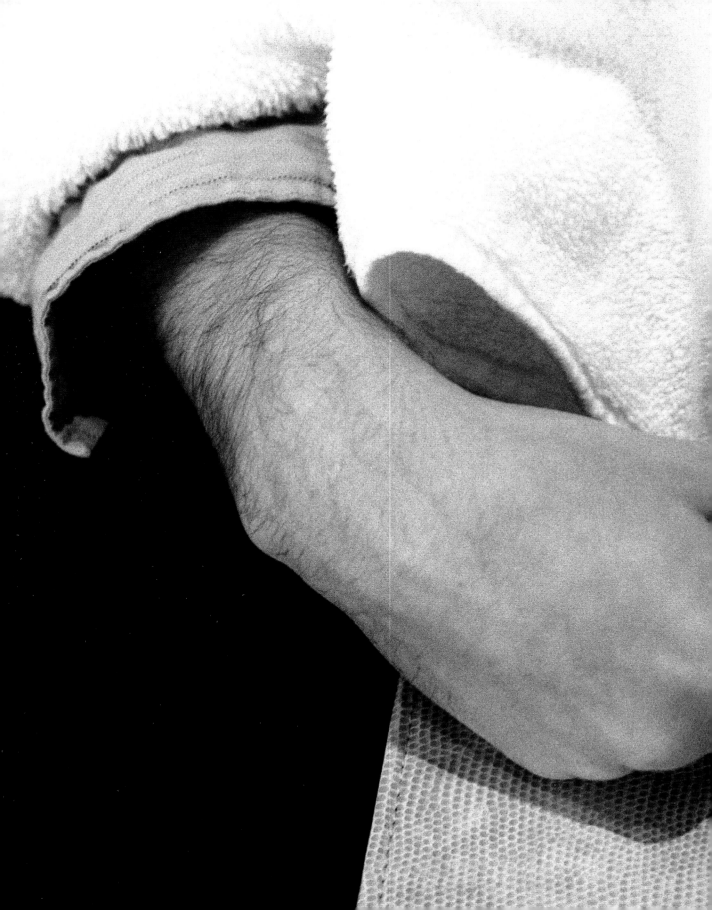

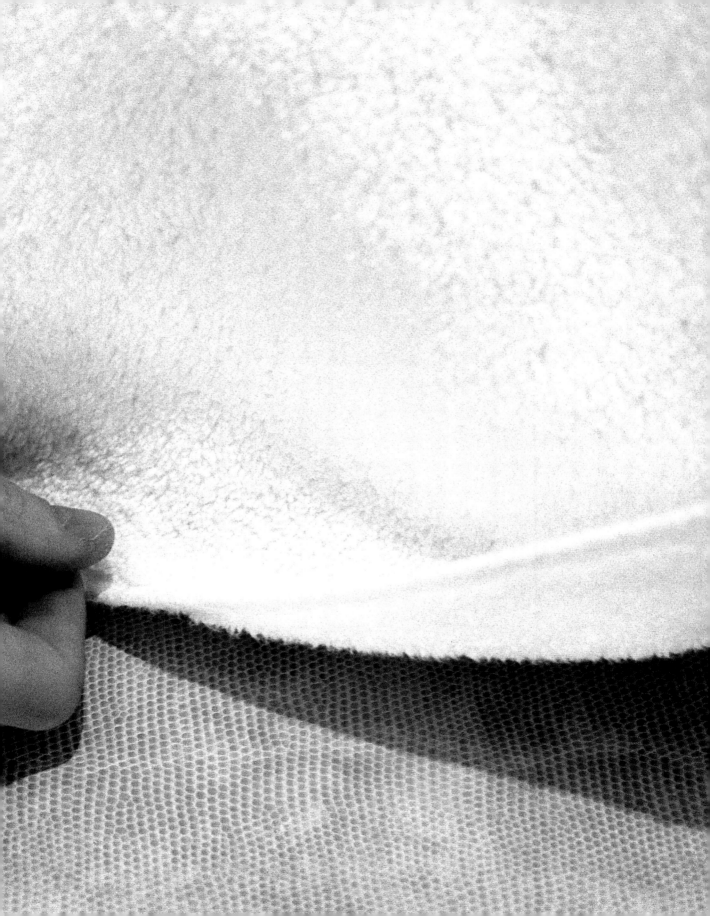

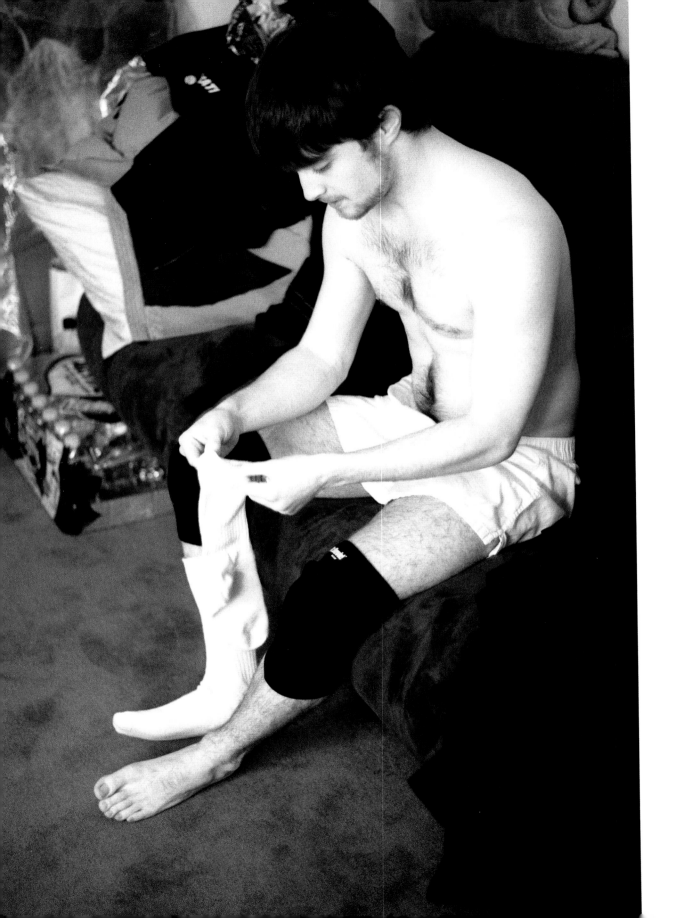

1054
"PRIMAL AND ELECTRIC!"
RICHARD
GRIFFITHS
EQUUS
BY PETER SHAFFER
Limited Engagement Ends Feb 8
Telecharge.com • 212.239.6200
Broadhurst Theatre, 235 W. 44th St.
FUEL 866.685.FUEL
icon
Park here
for all
Broadway
Shows

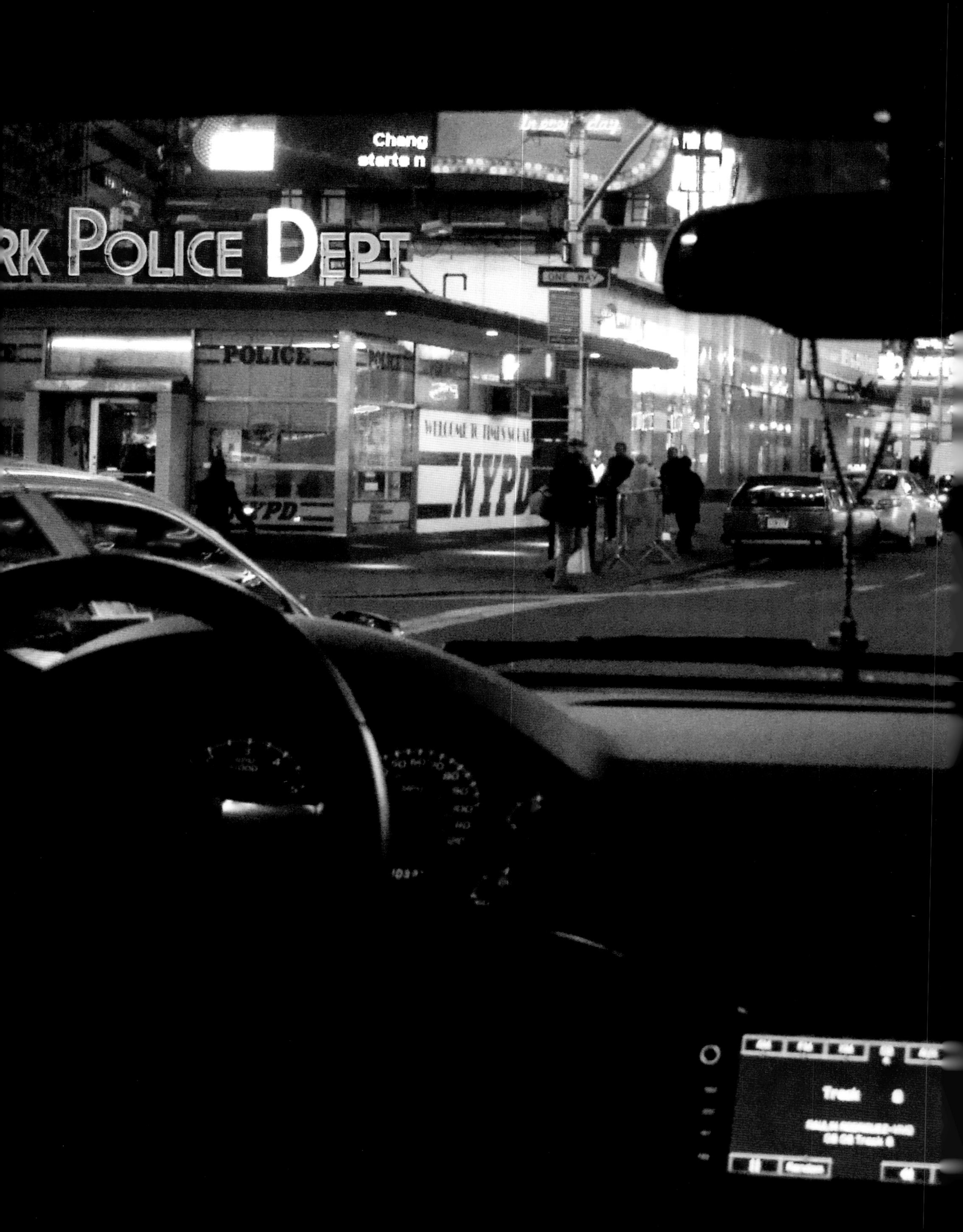
Chang
starts n
RK POLICE DEPT
ONE WAY
POLICE
NYPD
NYPD
Track

Notes on the Day
DANIEL RADCLIFFE

I always go to sleep at night with the television on. It helps me switch off. I must also have the remote control by my side at all times. During my time in NY I became totally hooked on all political programmes and loved coming back after a performance of EQUUS and watching The Colbert Report. Being in NY during the run up to the election was electrifying. I watched every single debate, every single analysis and loved how every moment was dissected and examined with forensic precision. The passion which leapt from the screen was contagious and I did find myself getting totally swept away on the tide of optimism which swept through America. On the actual Election Day I went to the voting station with a friend – it felt as if something significant was about to take place.

I love bed! It is a place to rest, dream, hide, worry, digest, analyze and fantasize. I would always stay in it for as long as I could, if I wasn't doing anything else during that day (which wasn't often). Monday was always our day off from performing EQUUS, so going to bed after the Sunday performance knowing that there was nothing to get up for the next day was bliss. During the holiday performance schedule - which was gruelling – it was wonderful to throw myself in bed at the end of the day.

The view from my bedroom window was always extraordinary. I loved looking over at New Jersey and watching the river traffic on the Hudson. The picture never stayed the same – colour, light, traffic, weather – forever changing - you never knew what was going

to appear next. In fact, on the extraordinary day when the U.S airways flight landed on the river, it floated right past the apartment. Fortunately no one was hurt, but it was a very eerie sight watching the events on television unfold in front of my bedroom window.

I found the river magical, haunting and very beautiful, particularly when it partially iced over.

I can spend hours in the shower. I sing a lot in the shower – warming up the voice – getting everything moving in preparation for the performance. The bathroom always looks as if it has been hit by a bomb – which is quite an achievement when you think about it as it really is usually only me and a couple of towels!

Cricket is one of my passions and one of the greatest inventions has to be Slingbox, as I was always able to keep up to date with my cricket scores and watch the matches being played around the world. I would literally have to be dragged away from my laptop to leave for the theatre on time, especially if England was playing.

Wherever I go, I must always have books with me. I travel with a library and keep adding to it wherever I am working. Being searched at airports is always an interesting experience as I resemble a mobile library. Working with Richard Griffiths was totally inspirational and every evening before we went on stage we would chat about books and Richard would recommend books that I should read and he would quote long passages from

some of his favourite novels. We would discuss poetry, plays, novels, musicals and always Richard would recount amazing tales about the authors we were discussing. To sit in his presence and listen to this incredible man was a huge privilege and one I will never forget.

During the run of EQUUS I inevitably did have a cold a couple of times and I would inhale an old fashioned remedy called Friars Balsam (recommended by my aunt) to clear my head. This is an old fashioned Northern Irish remedy that my aunt swears by. I arrived in NY with many bottles of this strange-smelling potion and it got me through many a challenging afternoon or evening performance, if I was suffering. There is nothing quite so unpleasant as being on stage and not being able to breathe!! But I was determined not to miss a performance. Only hospitalization would have prevented me from going on and thankfully that didn't happen.

As I was spending the afternoon of January 13th working with my voice coach I devoured a huge bowl of cheesey tuna pasta as this had to see me through until after the evening performance. This was also my staple diet on matinee days. Midweek matinees are peculiar beasts. I knew that once I left the apartment, I would be in the theatre for almost twelve hours, without leaving the building. So I would have a lunch that would get me through the matinee performance and I would spend the time gazing out of the window mentally preparing for the afternoon ahead.

The other thing I must travel with at all times is my dvd collection which, like my book collection, just gets bigger and bigger because I inevitably talk to someone who recommends a film, or a stand up comedian, or an old black and white film that I have never seen and the library keeps on growing.

More books. As I said, I go everywhere with them. They become companions. Books that have been recommended, books for reference, for amusement, for inspiration. I never travel anywhere without a least a dozen books – poetry books, novels, trivia books, plays - they all come with me.

The journey up the West Side Highway was never dull. I loved travelling into the theatre every day and I always thought of the great Cole Porter song
" I happen to like New York,
I happen to love this town
I like the city air, I like to drink of it
The more I see New York , the more I think of it
I like the sight and the sound and even the stink of it
I happen to like New York"

During the run of EQUUS I brought my voice coach, Barbara Houseman, out to NY to continue the process we had started eighteen months before I went into rehearsals in London for EQUUS. She is a truly inspirational lady and we continue to work together as new challenges present themselves.

Spase. My security guard in NY was the wonderful Spase from Macedonia. Protective,

highly efficient, thoughtful and very very funny! It always amused me because most people thought he was so intense and without humour. They were wrong. He is one of the kindest, most loyal people I have ever met. Not only did he look after me, but he looked after my many friends who travelled to NY from the UK. He is a big man who made a big impression on all my friends.

When I am away from home I keep in touch with my friends by text – travelling to the theatre was a great way to read what they were up to and for me to bring them up to date with the fun I was having in NY.

Arriving at the stage door- work begins!

I was always in the theatre very early. It was part of my preparation – I would go around and see as many of the actors in the theatre before we went on stage. During the rehearsal period you get to see everyone in the company all the time and you hear all the gossip, but as soon as a play opens the chances are you may not see them until you walk on stage. I don't like this, so once I had put on my knee protectors and jeans, I went to see everyone to catch up with all the company news. I loved going around every evening to catch up with what everyone had been up to during the day.

I am wearing a Giants t-shirt, which was given to me by all the stage-hands. As soon as I got to the theatre, I was converted to the Giants by the rabid football fans working there. Ronnie is the only long suffering Jets

fan of the Broadhurst Theatre crew and he never stopped trying to win me over to the white and green jersey of the Jets.

My dressing room table was always littered with books, silly toys and, did I mention books? At the beginning of the run my table was quite an ordered place to put things, but by the end, I had accumulated so many little trinkets that had been given to me by fans particularly plastic cowboys, it was a treasure trove of the weird and wonderful!!

One of the best things about being on Broadway was feeling part of the community. It was like nothing I had ever experienced before. An actor who works on Harry Potter and had been on Broadway did tell me before I left that I would be embraced by the community in a way I had never experienced before – and he was right. I made so many amazing friends during my time there. It was impossible not to throw myself into life on Broadway with gusto! During the run of EQUUS we helped to raise money for the amazing organisation Broadway Cares/ Equity Fights AIDS. For six weeks after each performance we would auction something from the show to help raise more money for this incredible organisation – everything from my sweaty t-shirt to an even sweatier pair of jeans. I am happy to report that EQUUS raised the most money this year – so thank you to everyone who contributed, when you came to see the show. We also took part in the 'Gypsy of The Year' competition where each show performs a skit – this was my first time singing and dancing on stage so I was completely terrified – it was amazing fun and

we came second to The Lion King's wonderful dance piece.

On my opening night this little note arrived with flowers from Patti Lupone – The Queen of Broadway! I was incredibly excited and flattered.

My favourite shoes – no laces! What joy for a lazy man.

Every week before the beginning of the show I would have a massage with our resident physical therapist. It was a chance to sort out the aches, pains, and stiffness that went with the show – only to get them all over again and again and…

The horses' masks that have haunted me on stage for almost a year! When I first saw these heads in London I thought they were quite beautiful but, once they are placed on the actors' heads they became completely menacing and disturbing.

Every Tuesday we would always gather and rehearse the blinding at the end of the play as the slightest error would have meant disaster. There were certainly a number of occasions when a hoof came just a bit too close for comfort – fortunately the wonderful actor dancers who played the horses were always completely aware of what was happening and would react with lightning speed.

People often ask me if I prefer theatre or film and it really is an impossible question to answer. What I discovered working in

the theatre both in London and NY was the sense of community that I absolutely loved. It was incredibly exciting every night to feel that, as one, we were facing an audience together. I love the fact that when you are on stage there is no place to hide – it doesn't matter how you feel, or what an awful day you have had, you have to go out there and perform. Your performance can't be changed in an edit suite, or a line that isn't clear be enhanced with re-recording. You, with the rest of the cast, are on the front line and there is nothing quite like the thrill of walking out on that stage to begin the assault.

After two and a half hours the curtain call comes. The first time I took a curtain call was in London after the first preview. Nothing had prepared me! I was so completely overwhelmed by the response from the audience that I could hardly walk across the stage. Fortunately, Richard was there to hold on to me and get me through it!

The amazing response we had night after night in New York was always exhilarating. EQUUS is an intense theatrical experience for an audience and for many people it was their first experience of theatre and a marvellous way to start a journey, on which I hope they continue.

EQUUS was truly a milestone in my life. When I first met Peter Shaffer in London I was completely overwhelmed to hear him talk about the play and its history. He is a truly wonderful writer and human being. He was also so generous to me with his time

and advice and I loved being in his company. When I first told people that I was going to be doing EQUUS the response was always the same – "That's the play that made me want to be an actor or a writer or a designer" It still remains a powerful theatrical experience and an important piece of theatre for so many people. I am thrilled to be part of its history.

This was one of the occasions that Barbara was with me during the run and here we are analyzing the evening's performance

Ignore the crutches in this photograph It was a First Night present from a good friend who has a rather black sense of humour You know the old phrase in theatre land about breaking a leg? They were just in case I did.

It takes several minutes for me to let the dust settle after a performance, just quietly thinking about it and mulling over the events on stage during that evening.

I always had to wait until the barriers were erected before I left the theatre, so there was a little time to play with my cricket ball!

It was my intention, every night, to sign at the stage door. This was always an interesting experience. Sometimes things got a little out of hand and the situation became unsafe because of the pushing a shoving that took place. I would have to be removed usually because security were concerned about safety in the crowd. This was always disappointing as people had been told no

to push but they didn't seem to realise that the safer the crowd, the longer I could have stayed out there. I was, however, always impressed by the fact that many people faced all sorts of extreme weather conditions to wait to get a signature. I always did as many as was possible and was staggered to hear that so many people had already seen the production in London and had come to see it again in New York.

On the day Tim was taking these photos we passed a poster in the garage, close to the theatre, and thought that it would make a fun photo, juxtaposing naked me with fully clothed me.

As we were heading home through Times Square, Tim suggested that we simply jump out and take a few quick shots, as it was pretty deserted (it was after all absolutely freezing). It really is an extraordinary place especially when it is empty. The glow of the red TKTS stairs gave an other- worldly quality to the picture. This is one of my favourites.

Heading home. After two shows it was always bliss to travel home – I used to love looking out the car window, thinking about what had happened during the day, and looking forward to getting into bed again for more rest and sleep before I did it all again tomorrow.

Back where I started!

More Colbert Report! More cricket scores! Watching the traffic on the Hudson and the lights of New Jersey. Good night!

Tim Hailand is eternally grateful to Dan Radcliffe – thanks for spending your day with me, allowing me to photograph you, and for your wonderful words. Special thanks to Spase Pejoski, Jim Hodges, Luis Lavienna, Tapio Snellman, Gordon Wise, Barbara Houseman, Felix Lora, Dennys Ilic, Chris Pomeroy, Frank Fratarolli, Nancy Wolff, Jake Shears, Jake Courtis, Stephen Galloway, Jil Derryberry, Vanessa Davies, Scott Boute, Anthony Meier, Tom Viola, Sam Rudy, Julian Calder, Julia Bowen and the entire cast, crew, and producers of EQUUS.

This book is dedicated to Caroline and Jack Hailand, Marcia Gresham and Alan Radcliffe, and in loving memory of Mona Hodges, who brought us all together.

Photography by Tim Hailand
Book design by Tim Hailand and Julian Calder Publishing
Packaged and produced by Julian Calder Publishing Ltd www.juliancalderpublishing.com
Printed by Jade Productions Hong Kong

 A portion of proceeds of every book sold is donated to Broadway Cares/Equity Fights AIDS - The nation's leading industry-based, non-profit AIDS fundraising and grant-making organizations. Since its founding in 1988, BC/EFA has raised over $160 million dollars for critically needed services for people with AIDS and other serious illnesses. For more information visit: www.BroadwayCares.org

To order additional copies of this book please visit: onedayinthelifeof.org

Published by HAILAND BOOKS